Legends and Stories

FROM THE CONTINENTAL DIVIDE TRAIL

STEVE STOCKTON
JASON KENT

FREE REIGN
Publishing

Contents

Introduction

In the vast, untamed wilderness of America, there is a world where the ordinary is transformed into the extraordinary, and the spirit of adventure intertwines with the echoes of ages past. I'm Steve Stockton, and together with my co-author Jason Kent, we've embarked on a journey of exploration and storytelling, bringing you *Legends and Stories: From the Continental Divide Trail.*

Before we ventured into the heart of the Continental Divide Trail (CDT), we had the privilege of uncovering the captivating narratives that shroud the Appalachian Trail and the Pacific Crest Trail. Those experiences left us mesmerized, eager to discover more untold stories and share them with fellow adventurers and enthusiasts.

Now, we invite you to join us on the CDT, a 3,100-mile odyssey that stretches from the deserts of New

Mexico to the remote wilderness of Glacier National Park in Montana. As we set foot on this trail, we immersed ourselves in a world where rugged landscapes and natural wonders served as the backdrop to an array of legends and stories, both ancient and modern.

The CDT is not just a physical path; it's a gateway to the very soul of America's wilderness. With each step, you'll encounter the whispers of Native American traditions, the tales of early explorers who charted these lands, and the enduring spirit of modern thru-hikers. You'll witness the ever-changing face of nature and the unique challenges that this trail presents, from the fierce storms of the Rocky Mountains to the solitary stretches of the Great Divide Basin.

So, lace up your hiking boots, pack your curiosity, and embark on this literary expedition through the untamed beauty and timeless tales that define the Continental Divide Trail. Prepare to be enthralled, enlightened, and inspired as you journey alongside Jason and me, as we guide you deeper into the wilderness and closer to the legends that call it home.

- Steve Stockton

One

THE CURSE OF THE GILA CLIFF DWELLINGS

IN THE REMOTE wilderness of southwestern New Mexico, where the Continental Divide Trail (CDT) winds its way through rugged terrain, a chilling legend has cast a shadow over the Gila Cliff Dwellings. This legend tells of a curse that haunts those who dare to disturb the ancient site. While some may dismiss it as folklore, others swear by its eerie power.

* * *

The Ancient Ruins:

The Gila Cliff Dwellings, located within the Gila Wilderness of southwestern New Mexico, are a remarkable archaeological site that offers a glimpse into the lives of the Mogollon people who inhabited this area over 700 years ago. The history of the Gila Cliff Dwellings can be divided into several key periods:

-**Construction and Occupation (circa 1275 CE):** The Gila Cliff Dwellings were constructed by the Mogollon people around 1275 CE. This ancient culture was known for its agricultural practices and skill in crafting pottery and baskets. The Mogollon constructed the cliff dwellings by using stone and clay mortar to create rooms and living spaces within the natural alcoves of the Gila Wilderness cliffs. It is estimated that the site was occupied for only a few decades, and the reasons for its abandonment remain a subject of archaeological study and speculation.

-**Rediscovery by European Americans (Late 19th Century):** The cliff dwellings remained hidden from European settlers until 1878 when a local rancher named Henry B. Ailman stumbled upon them. Ailman is often credited with the rediscovery of the site. Word of the remarkable cliff dwellings soon spread, attracting the attention of archaeologists, historians, and adventurers.

-**Archaeological Exploration (Late 19th to Early 20th Century):** The Gila Cliff Dwellings gained prominence as archaeologists began to explore the site in the late 19th and early 20th centuries. Some artifacts were removed from the site during these excavations, contributing to the legend of the curse associated with the cliff dwellings.

-**Preservation and Establishment as a National Monument (1907):** Concerns about the preservation of the site led to its designation as a National Monument by President Theodore Roosevelt in 1907. The Gila Cliff Dwellings National Monument was established to protect the archaeological remains and the unique architectural features of the dwellings.

-**Modern Research and Conservation:** In the decades that followed, ongoing archaeological research has provided valuable insights into the daily lives of the Mogollon people who once inhabited the cliff dwellings. Efforts have also been made to preserve and restore the structures, as well as to ensure that visitors can explore and learn from this exceptional site while respecting its historical and cultural significance.

* * *

The Curse:

The curse of the Gila Cliff Dwellings is said to have originated when the site was first excavated by modern archaeologists in the late 19th century. According to legend, an artifact was taken from the site, triggering a chain of misfortune. The curse is believed to bring bad luck, illness, and even death to those who remove any objects or disrupt the sacred grounds.

One of the most famous accounts associated with the curse is the story of an artifact collector named Emanuel Frey. In the early 20th century, Frey removed several artifacts from the Gila Cliff Dwellings, including pottery, tools, and religious items. Soon after, his life took a tragic turn. He experienced financial ruin, the death of family members, and illness. Convinced that the curse was responsible for his misfortunes, Frey returned the stolen artifacts to the site in an attempt to lift the curse.

Despite the passage of time, the legend of the Gila Cliff Dwellings curse persists. Many visitors to the site refuse to take even a pebble as a souvenir, fearing the curse's wrath. The National Park Service, which manages the site, actively discourages the removal of any artifacts, seeking to preserve the integrity of this remarkable archaeological treasure.

While the curse is a compelling legend, archaeologists and scientists have a different perspective. They argue that

Frey's misfortunes were coincidental and not the result of a curse. Instead, they emphasize the importance of preserving the Gila Cliff Dwellings as a historical and cultural site, respecting the artifacts left behind by the ancient Mogollon people.

The curse of the Gila Cliff Dwellings continues to capture the imaginations of visitors and researchers alike. Whether one believes in the curse or not, the site's historical and cultural significance is undeniable. As hikers and explorers journey along the Continental Divide Trail, they are reminded of the mysterious, eerie legend that lingers in the canyons and cliffs of this remote corner of New Mexico, leaving them to ponder the enigmatic stories of the past.

Two

THE GHOSTLY TALES OF THE SAN JUAN MOUNTAINS

THE SAN JUAN MOUNTAINS, nestled within the heart of the Rocky Mountains in southwestern Colorado, have long been shrouded in mystique and legend. Hikers on the Continental Divide Trail (CDT) who pass through this region are often captivated by the ghostly tales that swirl around these rugged peaks, valleys, and historic mining towns. In this chapter, we'll explore some of the factual accounts and encounters that contribute to the area's eerie reputation.

* * *

A Haunting Presence in Animas Forks:

One of the most iconic ghost towns in the San Juan Mountains is Animas Forks. It was established in 1873, following the discovery of silver and other valuable minerals in the area. It quickly grew into a thriving mining town, with a peak population of around 450 residents. The last family left Animas Forks in the 1920s, leaving it abandoned.

Visitors have reported disembodied voices, ghostly apparitions, and the sensation of being watched while exploring the decaying structures. Some have even captured mysterious figures in photographs, adding to the intrigue of this ghost town.

Situated at an elevation of 11,200 feet (3,414 meters), Animas Forks is one of the highest ghost towns in the United States. Its remote location made it accessible only during the summer months due to heavy snowfall in the winter.

* * *

The Legend of the Phantom Stagecoach:

In the heart of the San Juan Mountains, a legend that has been passed down through generations tells of a spectral stagecoach that traverses the old stagecoach road near the town of Silverton, Colorado. While some may dismiss it as mere folklore, the Legend of the Phantom Stagecoach is deeply ingrained in the region's history and has been experienced by those who have ventured into the rugged terrain along the Continental Divide Trail (CDT).

The stagecoach road near Silverton, Colorado, was once a vital transportation route during the 19th century mining boom. Stagecoaches carried miners, prospectors, and essential supplies to the remote mining camps in the San Juan Mountains. The area's harsh winters, treacherous terrain, and sudden blizzards made these journeys perilous, and not all travelers reached their destinations safely.

Witnesses who have reported encounters with the Phantom Stagecoach describe a ghostly scene. They've seen an old-fashioned stagecoach, complete with wooden wheels and a driver, materialize on the road in the dead of night. The horses that pull the coach are said to be ghostly and translucent, glowing with an eerie light.

One of the most chilling aspects of these encounters is

the sound. Witnesses claim to hear the thundering hooves of the ghostly horses and the rattling of the stagecoach wheels, even when the apparition itself is not visible. The noise is said to be deafening, echoing through the stillness of the mountain night.

The legend gains credence from the historical record, as there were numerous stagecoach accidents along this perilous route during the mining era. Many lives were lost due to harsh weather, avalanches, and accidents on the narrow mountain roads. These tragedies provide a haunting backdrop to the legend of the Phantom Stagecoach.

Over the years, there have been several reported sightings and encounters with the Phantom Stagecoach. These experiences often occur near the old stagecoach road, especially in the vicinity of Silverton. Witnesses range from hikers and tourists to seasoned locals who are well-acquainted with the legend.

Skeptics offer various explanations for the legend, including optical illusions, natural phenomena, and echoes from nearby mining operations. Still, those who have witnessed the phenomenon are adamant that what they saw and heard was beyond the realm of the ordinary.

Whether one believes it to be a spectral relic of a bygone era or an atmospheric quirk of the high-altitude terrain, there's no denying the profound impact it has on those who experience it. As hikers follow the Continental Divide Trail through this rugged and mystical landscape, they may find themselves drawn into the timeless tale of the phantom stagecoach that still roams the mountain roads of Silverton.

The Ghost of Ophir Pass:

Ophir Pass, a high mountain pass located in the San Juan Mountains of southwestern Colorado, is known not only for its stunning natural beauty but also for the enduring legend of the Ghost of Ophir Pass.

With an elevation of approximately 11,800 feet, Ophir Pass has played a significant role in the history of the San Juan Mountains. It was originally used by Ute Native Americans as a trading route, and later, during the late 19th century, it became a vital path for miners and prospectors seeking their fortunes in the region's rich mineral deposits.

Over the years, hikers, locals, and visitors to Ophir Pass have reported encountering a spectral figure in the vicinity. Descriptions of the apparition vary, but it is often described as a miner from the late 1800s, wearing tattered clothing and appearing as though he is trapped in the past. Witnesses have claimed to see this ghostly figure wandering along the pass, sometimes appearing lost or disoriented.

Legend has it that the ghost of Ophir Pass is the spirit of a miner who met a tragic end in the harsh and unforgiving conditions of the San Juan Mountains. While there are various versions of the story, one common thread is that this miner perished due to exposure, starvation, or a mining accident in the area. His spirit is said to linger on, unable to find peace or rest.

Several individuals who have hiked or explored Ophir Pass have shared accounts of eerie encounters with the ghostly miner. Some claim to have seen him at dusk or during the night, while others have reported hearing faint footsteps or voices when no one else was present. These experiences have left a lasting impression on those who have ventured into the pass.

As with many ghostly legends, there are those who approach the tale of the Ghost of Ophir Pass with skepticism. Some argue that the eerie encounters can be attributed to natural phenomena, psychological factors, or simply the power of suggestion. Nevertheless, the persistence of these stories suggests that they hold a unique place in the lore of Ophir Pass and the San Juan Mountains.

The Whispers of Silverton Cemetery:

While this cemetery serves as the final resting place for many residents of this former mining town, it has also gained notoriety for the eerie and unsettling experiences reported by visitors.

Silverton, Colorado, was founded in 1874 during the peak of the mining boom in the San Juan Mountains. Hillside Cemetery, established in 1876, became the burial ground for many early pioneers, miners, and their families. Its historical significance, combined with the striking beauty of the surrounding landscape, draws both tourists and history enthusiasts to this remote location.

Visitors to Hillside Cemetery have consistently reported unusual experiences. Among the most common are accounts of faint whispers and soft laughter, often heard while wandering among the tombstones. These whispers are often described as unintelligible, making it difficult to discern their source. Some claim that these voices carry an otherworldly quality, leaving them with an uncanny feeling that they are not alone.

In an age of smartphone cameras and digital photography, some visitors have captured peculiar anomalies in their photographs taken at Hillside Cemetery. These anomalies range from unexplained orbs of light to misty apparitions seemingly hovering near the gravesites. While skeptics attribute these phenomena to lens flares or dust particles, believers find them compelling evidence of the cemetery's haunted reputation.

The source of these whispers and eerie phenomena remains a topic of speculation among both locals and paranormal enthusiasts. Some believe that the voices are the echoes of those interred in the cemetery, their spirits lingering in this tranquil resting place. Others suggest that the wind rustling through the nearby pines may create the auditory illusions, but this theory does not account for the specificity of the whispers.

Despite the unsettling stories, Hillside Cemetery is also cherished for its serenity and breathtaking views of the surrounding mountains. It has become a place of reflection and remembrance for those with loved ones buried here. The juxtaposition of its haunting reputation with its natural beauty only adds to the allure of this historic burial ground.

For hikers on the Continental Divide Trail passing through Silverton, a visit to Hillside Cemetery can be a unique and slightly eerie experience. It offers a glimpse into the town's rich history and the enduring mysteries that shroud this quiet corner of Colorado.

While the whispers of Silverton Cemetery may defy easy explanation, they remain an integral part of the cemetery's allure and contribute to the ongoing fascination with this atmospheric location along the Continental Divide Trail.

The Mysterious Vanishing Cabin:

Amidst the rugged and remote terrain of Stony Pass on the Continental Divide Trail (CDT), there exists a peculiar and enigmatic phenomenon—the Mysterious Vanishing Cabin. Hikers and adventurers who have traversed this region have reported eerie encounters with a cabin that seemingly appears and disappears at will.

The earliest accounts of the Mysterious Vanishing Cabin date back several decades. Hikers who ventured through the Stony Pass area began sharing stories of a secluded cabin they stumbled upon during their journeys. These encounters raised questions about the cabin's origins, as it appeared to be in a state of disrepair yet devoid of any signs of recent habitation.

One of the most perplexing aspects of the Mysterious Vanishing Cabin is its inconsistent location. Hikers have described coming across the cabin on various parts of the trail, often with no discernible pattern. Some have reported finding it at higher elevations, while others swear they encountered it closer to Stony Pass itself. This inconsistency has left many baffled.

What truly sets this mystery apart is the cabin's propensity to vanish without a trace. Hikers who have explored the cabin one day have returned to the same spot on subsequent hikes, only to find no remnants of the structure. It's as though the cabin itself possesses an other-worldly quality, appearing and disappearing at its own discretion.

Skeptics and rationalists argue that the cabin's apparent vanishing act can be attributed to environmental factors, such as avalanches, rockslides, or even shifting soil. Such natural occurrences could feasibly bury or destroy the cabin temporarily, only to expose it again at a later time. However, this theory doesn't account for the fact that hikers have reported encountering the cabin in varying states of disrepair over the years.

Despite attempts to explain away the phenomenon, the Mysterious Vanishing Cabin continues to intrigue hikers and adventurers along the CDT. Some speculate that the cabin may be a mirage or a manifestation of the wilderness itself, while others entertain the idea that it is a portal to another realm, appearing and disappearing as it connects with different dimensions.

Over the years, several hikers have documented their encounters with the Mysterious Vanishing Cabin through photographs and written accounts. These records serve as a testament to the authenticity of the phenomenon and add to the mystique surrounding it.

The Ghostly Lights of La Garita Wilderness:

The La Garita Wilderness, a remote and rugged expanse is renowned not only for its stunning natural beauty but also for a mysterious phenomenon that has baffled and captivated observers for generations: the ghostly lights of La Garita.

The ghostly lights of La Garita Wilderness are unexplained, eerie lights that appear in the night sky above the wilderness. These lights have been described as glowing orbs, mysterious flames, or flickering lanterns, and they have been observed by hikers, campers, and residents of the area. The phenomenon is often associated with the vicinity of the Continental Divide Trail (CDT), which traverses through this wilderness area.

Several firsthand accounts exist from individuals who claim to have witnessed these enigmatic lights. While many of these accounts are anecdotal, they are consistent in their descriptions of the lights' behavior. Witnesses have reported seeing the lights dance, flicker, and move erratically through the sky, sometimes disappearing and reappearing. They are often described as having an otherworldly, ethereal quality.

The phenomenon of the ghostly lights of La Garita has a long history. Stories of these lights date back to the indigenous Ute people, who inhabited the region long before European settlers arrived. The Ute people considered the lights to be sacred and a sign of spiritual presence.

Despite numerous sightings and historical accounts, scientists have yet to provide a definitive explanation for the ghostly lights of La Garita. Some theories include:

- **Bioluminescent Organisms:** Some suggest that the lights may be caused by bioluminescent organisms or gases in the atmosphere, although this explanation doesn't entirely account for the lights' behavior.
- **Natural Gas Emissions:** Others propose that methane or other natural gases escaping from the Earth's crust could ignite and produce the lights. However, this theory is challenged by the lights' apparent ability to move and hover.
- **Atmospheric Phenomena:** Atmospheric conditions, such as temperature inversions and reflections from distant sources, have also been suggested as potential explanations. However,

these factors do not account for all observed characteristics of the lights.

While scientific investigations and theories persist, no conclusive explanation has been reached. As a result, these lights remain an enduring enigma, adding an extra layer of intrigue to an already captivating wilderness along the Continental Divide Trail. Whether they are the result of natural phenomena or something more mysterious, the ghostly lights of La Garita Wilderness continue to be a source of wonder and curiosity for all who encounter them.

The Legend of the Wild Man:

The Legend of the "Wild Man" of the San Juan Mountains is a local folklore story and urban legend associated with the San Juan Mountains in southwestern Colorado. This legend is not based on any confirmed historical events or real-life sightings but is rather a part of the region's folklore and storytelling tradition.

According to the legend, there is said to be a mysterious and reclusive figure known as the "Wild Man" or "Mountain Man" who inhabits the remote and rugged wilderness of the San Juan Mountains. The character is often depicted as a rugged and solitary individual who lives off the land, eschewing modern civilization. Some versions of the legend suggest that the Wild Man has been living in the mountains for years, avoiding contact with others and leaving behind only vague traces of his presence.

The legend likely draws from a combination of factors, including the area's history of early pioneers and prospectors who lived in isolation, the rugged and challenging terrain of the San Juan Mountains, and the allure of wilderness survival stories. Local folklore often incorporates elements of mystery and intrigue, adding to the mystique of the region.

It's important to emphasize that the Legend of the Wild Man is not based on factual accounts or documented sightings. Instead, it has become a storytelling tradition passed down through generations, adding a sense of adventure and wonder to the San Juan Mountains. While the legend contributes to the cultural heritage of the region, there is no concrete evidence to support the existence of such a figure.

In essence, the Wild Man of the San Juan Mountains is a part of the folklore and mythology that enriches the history and cultural fabric of the area, but it should be viewed as a story rather than a verified fact.

* * *

While skeptics may dismiss these accounts as products of overactive imaginations or natural phenomena, the ghostly tales of the San Juan Mountains persist, weaving an unsettling tapestry of mystery and intrigue for those who venture into this remote and hauntingly beautiful region along the Continental Divide Trail. Whether one believes in the supernatural or not, the stories of the San Juans continue to be an integral part of the trail's rich tapestry.

Three

THE PHANTOM TRAIN OF MARSHALL PASS, COLORADO

NESTLED amidst the rugged terrain of Colorado's Rocky Mountains is one of the most intriguing tales associated with this region and that is of the Phantom Train of Marshall Pass, a ghostly echo from the past that continues to captivate the imagination of locals and hikers alike.

Sitting at an elevation of 10,842 feet, Marshall Pass was once a critical transportation corridor in the late 19th and early 20th centuries. The Denver and Rio Grande Western Railroad laid tracks across this treacherous terrain, connecting the eastern and western parts of the state. The railroad was an engineering marvel of its time, navigating steep grades, sharp curves, and the harsh mountain environment.

As time marched on, the importance of the railroad diminished. The advent of more efficient transportation routes and the decline of mining activities in the region led to the eventual abandonment of the tracks in the 1950s. Nature began to reclaim the area, leaving behind remnants of tunnels, trestles, and railbeds.

It was in the wake of this abandonment that the legend of the Phantom Train of Marshall Pass began to take shape. Travelers, hikers, and locals reported hearing the distant sounds of a train chugging along the old tracks, accompanied by the haunting whistle echoing through the mountains. These auditory phenomena have been reported both during the day and at night, often described as eerily clear and unmistakably reminiscent of a bygone era.

Skeptics and enthusiasts alike have ventured into the area to uncover the source of these phantom sounds. Some propose that the reports are a result of acoustic anomalies, with natural sounds from the surrounding environment being distorted and amplified through the mountainous terrain. Others suggest that what people are hearing might be the residual sounds from active train lines situated further away, carried over long distances by the wind.

Despite the potential rational explanations, the allure of the Phantom Train of Marshall Pass remains strong. The story has become an integral part of local folklore, capturing the imagination of those who hear about it. For some, the phantom sounds serve as a haunting reminder of the past, a ghostly imprint left behind by the steam engines that once conquered the Rockies.

As the CDT continues to draw hikers from around the world, the tale of the Phantom Train of Marshall Pass endures as a piece of the trail's rich tapestry of stories. Whether regarded as a mere acoustic anomaly or embraced as a supernatural phenomenon, the legend stands testament to the enduring power of mystery and folklore in the heart of the Rockies.

THE GHOSTLY PHENOMENA OF STONEWALL PASS

STONEWALL PASS, nestled within the Sangre de Cristo Mountains of New Mexico, is a location rich in history and natural beauty. While it is renowned for its eerie and mysterious phenomena, its history extends far beyond these modern legends.

* * *

Stonewall Pass traverses the spine of the Rocky Mountains from Canada to Mexico. At an elevation of over 11,000 feet (3,352 meters), it is a challenging section for hikers and backpackers due to its steep terrain, unpredictable weather, and isolation. The pass itself is part of the larger Carson National Forest.

Long before European settlers arrived, the region surrounding Stonewall Pass was inhabited by indigenous peoples, including the Jicarilla Apache and Ute tribes. These Native American communities relied on the land for sustenance and spiritual significance. The area's natural beauty and resources made it an essential part of their lives.

During the late 19th and early 20th centuries, the Stonewall Pass area saw a flurry of mining activity, characteristic of the American West. Rich deposits of minerals such as gold, silver, and copper attracted prospectors and settlers to the region. Towns like Stonewall and nearby Cimarron thrived as mining communities.

The history of the Wild West, complete with saloons, shootouts, and boom-and-bust cycles, played out in the nearby towns. Some of the remnants of these mining operations and the communities they supported can still be found in the area.

The Continental Divide Trail, which includes

Stonewall Pass as one of its challenging sections, was officially designated in 1978. It follows the continental divide, providing hikers with the opportunity to experience the diverse landscapes and ecosystems that make up the Rocky Mountains. Stonewall Pass is a key waypoint along this epic trail, offering stunning vistas and access to the high alpine environment.

Ghostly Phenomena:

Stonewall Pass has earned a reputation for its mysterious and eerie occurrences. While some may attribute these phenomena to natural causes or the power of suggestion, the accounts of hikers and explorers who have encountered the unusual events at Stonewall Pass cannot be easily dismissed.

Hikers passing through Stonewall Pass have frequently reported hearing peculiar and inexplicable sounds echoing through the canyon. These sounds range from eerie whispers and distant laughter to unidentifiable voices, often seeming to emanate from the surrounding rock formations. While some suggest that these sounds might be the result of wind or natural acoustics, the distinct and human-like nature of the noises has left many unsettled.

One of the more chilling accounts involves the sighting

of a phantom campfire in the vicinity of Stonewall Pass. Hikers have claimed to see the flickering glow of a campfire at night, only to approach and find no source of light or heat. Some speculate that this ghostly campfire may be linked to the spirits of long-departed travelers who once sought warmth and refuge in the pass.

Several hikers have reported seeing shadowy figures or ghostly apparitions moving among the rocks and trees near Stonewall Pass. These encounters often occur during the twilight hours or in the early morning, when the pass is shrouded in darkness. Witnesses describe feeling an over-whelming sense of unease and dread during these spectral encounters.

Stonewall Pass is known for its unique wind patterns that seem to whisper secrets to those who pass through. Some hikers have claimed to hear faint but distinct voices carried by the wind, as though the very breeze itself is conveying messages. While these phenomena may be attributed to the play of air currents through the pass, they contribute to the pass's reputation as an eerie and haunted location.

Visitors to Stonewall Pass have reported feeling disoriented and experiencing time lapses or missing periods of time during their journey through the area. These sensations have left some hikers bewildered and questioning their own perception of reality.

As with many locations that have gained a reputation for ghostly phenomena, there are numerous theories about the causes of these events at Stonewall Pass. Some suggest that the unique geology and acoustic properties of the pass may play a role, while others believe that the pass holds a spiritual significance for the indigenous peoples of the region. Skeptics, of course, offer explanations rooted in natural phenomena.

While it's difficult to definitively explain the ghostly phenomena of Stonewall Pass, the accounts of those who have experienced these eerie events are an essential part of the lore and mystique surrounding this particular stretch of the Continental Divide Trail. Whether one attributes these occurrences to the supernatural or natural causes, the ghostly reputation of Stonewall Pass endures as a source of fascination and intrigue for those who explore its rugged terrain.

Five

LA LLORONA - THE WEEPING WOMAN

THE LEGEND of La Llorona finds its roots in the Hispanic and Indigenous cultures of the American Southwest, particularly in New Mexico. The tale speaks of a beautiful woman named Maria, who, driven by jealousy and rage, drowns her two children in a river after being spurned by their father. Upon realizing the gravity of her actions, Maria is consumed by grief and drowns herself.

The story goes that Maria's soul is trapped between the living and the dead, condemned to wander the riverbanks, searching for her lost children. She is described as wearing a white or black gown, with long flowing hair, and her cries of "¡Ay, mis hijos!" ("Oh, my children!") are said to be heard along the rivers, especially at night.

In New Mexico, the legend of La Llorona has been woven into the cultural tapestry of the state, serving as a cautionary tale, a ghost story, and a part of the local identity. The Rio Grande, which runs through the heart of New Mexico, is often cited as a location where La Llorona might be encountered.

While the core elements of the La Llorona story remain consistent, there are numerous variations and interpretations of the tale. Some versions highlight the themes of love, betrayal, and tragedy, while others focus on the supernatural elements and the idea of La Llorona as a harbinger or an omen.

In some interpretations, La Llorona is seen as a symbol of grief and the consequences of one's actions, serving as a moral lesson on the importance of responsibility and the dangers of succumbing to anger or jealousy. In other versions, she is portrayed as a more malicious entity, seeking to harm or steal away children who wander too close to the riverbanks at night.

Over the years, there have been numerous reported encounters with La Llorona in New Mexico, especially in rural areas or near rivers. These accounts often describe eerie wailing, sightings of a ghostly figure near the water, or a sudden chill in the air.

For many in New Mexico, La Llorona is more than just a ghost story; she is a part of the cultural heritage, a spectral presence that lingers in the shadows of folklore. Whether one believes in the literal existence of La Llorona or views her as a symbolic figure, her legend undeniably adds a layer of mystery and depth to the narratives of New Mexico and the Continental Divide Trail.

In recent years, the legend of La Llorona has transcended its folkloric roots, entering the realms of literature, film, and popular culture. However, in New Mexico, she remains a potent and enduring figure, a ghostly echo of the past that continues to captivate the imagination and evoke the emotions of those who hear her tale.

As hikers traverse the rugged terrains of the Continental Divide Trail, they step into a landscape rich in stories and legends, where the cries of La Llorona might just be carried on the winds, a haunting reminder of the tales that have shaped and defined the region for centuries.

THE LEGEND OF THE WHITE SANDS SIRENS

THE WHITE SANDS NATIONAL MONUMENT, located in southern New Mexico, is a unique and otherworldly landscape of white gypsum sand dunes covering approximately 275 square miles. Its history is both fascinating and intertwined with natural processes, indigenous cultures, military activities, and scientific research.

* * *

Long before European settlers arrived, the region was inhabited by indigenous peoples, including the Mescalero Apache and Tularosa Basin tribes. These indigenous communities had cultural and spiritual connections to the land, considering it sacred and rich with resources.

In the late 16th century, Spanish explorers, including Francisco Vásquez de Coronado, ventured through the region while searching for the mythical Seven Cities of Gold. However, they didn't recognize the potential significance of the gypsum dunes.

In the 19th century, the Tularosa Basin became a popular area for ranching and farming. Settlers often referred to the white dunes as "Alkali Flats" and faced challenges due to the harsh desert conditions.

In the early 20th century, the potential of the White Sands area as a military training ground was recognized. Lieutenant Colonel George S. Patton led a "Dunewood Experiment" in 1914, which involved testing military vehicles and equipment on the dunes. This experiment marked the beginning of the area's association with military activities.

In 1945, after World War II, the White Sands Proving Ground was established. It played a pivotal role in missile and rocket development, including the testing of the V-2 rocket under Operation Paperclip. Prominent scientists like Wernher von Braun conducted research there, laying the foundation for the U.S. space program.

White Sands National Monument was officially designated as such in 1933. The White Sands Missile Range, a military installation, surrounds the monument but allows for limited public access.

White Sands continues to be a site of scientific research, particularly in the fields of geology, ecology, and atmospheric studies. The monument's natural processes, such as dune formation and migration, are of interest to scientists.

The Tale of the Sirens:

As hikers traverse the Continental Divide Trail (CDT) through the vast deserts of New Mexico, they may come across a peculiar legend that adds an air of mystery to the already remote and unforgiving landscape. The Legend of The White Sands Sirens has been whispered among adventurers and locals alike, and though it may seem fantastical, it has a distinct presence along this section of the trail.

The Legend of The White Sands Sirens centers around the White Sands National Monument, a sprawling gypsum dune field in southern New Mexico. According to local lore, the White Sands Sirens are ethereal beings who inhabit the dunes, appearing as shimmering, ghostly figures. These spectral entities are said to be enchanting and captivating, luring unsuspecting travelers into the heart of the desert.

While some dismiss the legend as a mere superstition, others have reported eerie encounters with these supposed Sirens. Hikers and visitors to White Sands National Monument have described hearing hauntingly beautiful music or faint, alluring voices on the wind, often when they are wandering the dunes alone. These experiences leave a lasting impression, creating an atmosphere of both wonder and unease.

Rational explanations for the legend of the White Sands Sirens exist, rooted in the unique geological and atmospheric conditions of the area. The gypsum sand dunes can create peculiar acoustic effects, amplifying sounds and causing them to carry across vast distances. This phenomenon may explain the mysterious music and voices reported by hikers.

The Legend of The White Sands Sirens holds cultural significance for the local indigenous communities, including the Mescalero Apache Tribe. In their traditions, the Sirens are considered protectors of the land, and their presence is respected and revered. The legend serves as a reminder of the deep connection between the indigenous peoples and the unique natural features of the region.

While the notion of supernatural beings luring travelers into the desert may seem far-fetched, the legend of the White Sands Sirens persists, adding an aura of enchantment and intrigue to the already mystical landscape of the Continental Divide Trail in southern New Mexico. Hikers who venture through this area may find themselves captivated not only by the breathtaking dunes but also by the enduring allure of this intriguing legend.

LOST TREASURE

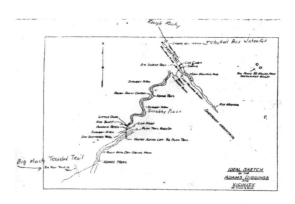

IN THE ANNALS of Continental Divide Trail history, there exists a captivating and persistent legend that has lured adventurers and treasure hunters for generations: the mystery of lost treasure hidden along the trail. While these tales may have their origins in actual historical events, they've been shrouded in mystery, with many seeking to uncover the elusive riches that supposedly lie hidden within the vast wilderness. Here, we delve into the factual information surrounding these stories, separated from the layers of fiction and speculation.

The Lost Adams Diggings:

One of the most enduring treasure legends along the CDT is that of the Lost Adams Diggings. According to the legend, in the 1860s, a prospector named Adams discovered an incredibly rich gold deposit somewhere in the mountains of New Mexico, near the CDT. He was said to have made a map, but after suffering from various misfortunes, he died before revealing the location of his find. Despite numerous searches, the exact location of the Lost Adams Diggings has never been confirmed, and it remains one of the most sought-after treasures along the CDT.

The legend of the Lost Adams Diggings is primarily associated with a man named Adams, although his full name and identity remain uncertain. Adams is said to have been a prospector who, in the 1860s, stumbled upon an incredibly rich gold deposit in the rugged and remote mountains of New Mexico.

According to the legend, Adams, realizing the immense value of his discovery, created a detailed map or left behind clues to the location of the gold deposit. However, before he could reveal the exact location to others, Adams faced a series of misfortunes, including illness and attacks by hostile Native American tribes.

The tale takes a dark turn with Adams' unexplained disappearance. Some versions of the story suggest that he may have been killed by the Apache or Comanche tribes, while others claim he died of illness or other causes. Regardless of the circumstances, Adams allegedly died without revealing the location of the gold.

Over the years, treasure hunters and adventurers have embarked on quests to locate the Lost Adams Diggings, driven by the belief that they could decipher the cryptic clues left by Adams. Numerous expeditions and searches have been conducted in the hopes of finding the treasure, but to date, no definitive proof of its existence has been uncovered.

The Lost Adams Diggings has become a part of the folklore and legend of the American Southwest, captivating the imaginations of those who hear the tale. Some versions of the story involve supernatural elements, curses, and the idea that the gold is guarded by restless spirits.

Despite the passage of time, the legend endures, and various theories and speculations persist regarding the possible location of the treasure. Treasure hunters and amateur historians continue to be drawn to the CDT region of New Mexico in search of the Lost Adams Diggings, making it an enduring mystery along the trail.

It's important to note that while the legend of the Lost Adams Diggings is a captivating story, the actual existence of such a treasure remains unverified, and many consider it to be more of a folklore tale than a historical fact. Nonetheless, the legend continues to contribute to the mystique and allure of the Continental Divide Trail and the surrounding wilderness.

The Fenn Treasure:

The Fenn Treasure, a real-life modern-day treasure hunt, captivated the public's imagination and led adventurers on a quest to uncover a hidden treasure chest filled with valuable artifacts and gold coins.

In 2010, Forrest Fenn, a wealthy art dealer, author, and former fighter pilot, claimed to have hidden a bronze chest filled with gold coins, jewelry, gemstones, and other valuable items somewhere in the Rocky Mountains. Fenn stated that the treasure chest weighed about 20 pounds and was hidden to inspire exploration of the outdoors and provide an adventure for treasure seekers.

Fenn provided a set of cryptic clues to the treasure's location in his memoir, "The Thrill of the Chase," which was published in 2010. The book contains a poem with nine clues meant to lead treasure hunters to the chest's hiding place.

Fenn specified that the treasure was hidden somewhere in the Rocky Mountains, spanning an area across several states, including New Mexico, Colorado, Wyoming, and Montana. The precise location was to be deduced from the clues in the poem.

In the years following the announcement of the treasure hunt, thousands of treasure hunters embarked on expeditions to decipher the clues and locate the chest. Many enthusiasts became obsessed with solving the puzzle and dedicated considerable time and resources to the search.

Tragically, several individuals lost their lives or faced dangerous situations while searching for the Fenn Treasure. This led to calls for Fenn to end the treasure hunt, as it was believed to be placing people in harm's way. Fenn defended the hunt, emphasizing that it was meant to be safe if approached responsibly.

On June 6, 2020, Forrest Fenn announced that the treasure had been found by an anonymous individual from "back East." He provided photographs of the recovered chest as proof. The exact location of the discovery was not disclosed to protect the finder's privacy, but it was revealed to be in the mountains of Wyoming.

Independent confirmation of the treasure's discovery came from Jack Stuef, a Michigan-based medical student, who came forward as the finder of the chest in December 2020. Stuef provided details about the location and the process of discovering the treasure, including his use of Fenn's clues.

The discovery of the Fenn Treasure put an end to the decade-long treasure hunt and added a real-life conclusion to a story that had enthralled adventurers and puzzle solvers alike. Forrest Fenn passed away in September 2020, and the treasure's existence and discovery remain documented facts in the annals of modern-day treasure hunting.

The Cursed Gold of Deadman's Gulch:

The legend of the Cursed Gold of Deadman's Gulch is a mysterious and enduring tale associated with the Continental Divide Trail (CDT), specifically in the San Juan Mountains of Colorado.

The legend of the Cursed Gold of Deadman's Gulch is intertwined with the history of gold mining in Colorado during the late 19th century. It is said that a prospector or group of miners in the San Juan Mountains made a significant gold discovery, and the exact location of this find was either kept secret or lost over time. This discovery is often associated with Deadman's Gulch, a real geographic feature in the area.

The legend holds that the gold found in Deadman's Gulch is cursed, and those who attempt to claim it will face dire consequences. These consequences could range from personal misfortune to untimely death. Such curses and superstitions were not uncommon in the mining communities of the American West during this era.

Different versions of the story exist, with variations in the number of prospectors involved, the size of the treasure, and the nature of the curse. Some accounts attribute the curse to the wrath of indigenous spirits or to the miners' disregard for the land and environment.

The legend of the Cursed Gold of Deadman's Gulch has attracted modern-day treasure hunters and enthusiasts who have sought to uncover the lost treasure. While some may dismiss the curse as superstition, others have reported strange and unsettling experiences while searching for the gold in the remote and rugged terrain of the San Juan Mountains.

During the late 19th century, Colorado experienced a significant gold rush, with prospectors flocking to the region in search of riches. This period marked the height of mining activity in the San Juan Mountains, and many fortunes were made and lost in the pursuit of precious metals.

While the legend of the Cursed Gold of Deadman's Gulch remains steeped in mystery and folklore, no confirmed historical records or documented discoveries of the cursed treasure exist. It serves as a reminder of the allure and intrigue associated with the untamed wilderness and the stories that have become intertwined with the history of the Continental Divide Trail.

The Legend of Spanish Conquistadors:

The legend of Spanish Conquistadors burying treasures in the American Southwest, including areas near the Continental Divide Trail (CDT), is a well-known folklore and part of the broader legend of "Lost Treasures of the Southwest." While there is some historical basis for the presence of Spanish explorers in the region during the 16th and 17th centuries, the specifics of hidden treasures are largely unverified and have taken on mythic proportions.

During the period of Spanish colonization in the Americas, explorers and Conquistadors ventured into what is now the southwestern United States, including states like New Mexico and Arizona. They were in search of riches, including gold and silver, and established missions and settlements throughout the region. This historical context forms the basis for the legend of buried treasure.

The legend suggests that Spanish Conquistadors, while exploring the American Southwest, came across vast amounts of gold, silver, and other valuable treasures. Fearing attacks by Indigenous peoples or rival European powers, some Conquistadors were said to have buried these riches in remote and hidden locations.

Over the years, treasure hunters and adventurers have pursued these legends, leading expeditions and conducting searches for the hidden treasures. They often rely on historical accounts, maps, and folklore to guide their efforts. The legend has been popularized in books, movies, and documentaries.

Despite decades of searching, no conclusive evidence of vast buried treasures from the Conquistador era has been found in the American Southwest. While some smaller caches of Spanish artifacts have been discovered, the existence of massive hidden treasures remains speculative.

The Cursed Treasure of Victorio Peak:

Nestled within the rugged terrains of New Mexico,

Victorio Peak holds a mystery that has perplexed treasure hunters, historians, and adventurers for decades. The peak, named after the Apache chief Victorio, is surrounded by stories of hidden treasures, lost fortunes, and a curse that has left many empty-handed and bewildered.

The story of Victorio Peak's hidden treasure dates back to 1937 when a local man named Doc Noss went deer hunting in the Hembrillo Basin. According to the lore, Noss stumbled upon a hidden entrance to a series of tunnels within Victorio Peak. Inside, he claimed to have discovered a staggering amount of gold bars, coins, and artifacts, believed to be remnants of Spanish explorers or hidden wealth from the Apache tribe.

Noss's discovery soon turned into a tale of greed, mystery, and tragedy. Eager to capitalize on his find, Noss began to extract the gold, one piece at a time. However, he became increasingly paranoid and secretive, leading to estrangement from his wife, Ova Noss. In a twist of fate, Noss was shot and killed in 1949 during a dispute over the treasure. The location of the entrance to the treasure trove went to the grave with him, leaving the riches lost once again.

Complicating the search for Victorio Peak's treasure was its location within the White Sands Missile Range, a highly secured military facility. Access to the peak became restricted, fueling conspiracy theories and speculation about the military's involvement in the treasure hunt. Some believed that the government had located and extracted the treasure, while others speculated that it remained hidden within the peak, guarded by the curse and the military's watchful eye.

In the years following Noss's death, various individuals and groups have sought permission to search for the treasure at Victorio Peak. The most notable of these was a 1977 expedition led by Ova Noss's grandchildren, with the military's consent. Despite extensive efforts, including the use of metal detectors and excavation equipment, the treasure remained elusive, adding to the legend's mystique.

Skeptics of the Victorio Peak treasure argue that the story is a fabrication or that Noss might have exaggerated the extent of his find. Geologists have pointed out that the geological formations of Victorio Peak make the existence of such a vast treasure trove unlikely. Critics also highlight the lack of concrete evidence, such as photographs or verifiable artifacts, to substantiate the claims of a hidden treasure.

The tale of Victorio Peak's cursed treasure remains one of New Mexico's most enduring mysteries, captivating the imaginations of treasure hunters, historians, and adventure seekers alike. Whether the peak conceals a hidden fortune or simply a tantalizing legend, the story of Doc Noss and the elusive treasure has become an integral part of the folklore surrounding the Continental Divide Trail. The mystery of Victorio Peak continues to intrigue, serving as a testament to the human spirit's fascination with the unknown and the allure of lost riches.

Lost Cabin Gold Mine:

Nestled within the rugged expanse of Wyoming's Wind River Range, is the tale of the Lost Cabin Gold Mine, an elusive treasure said to be hidden deep within the wilderness, its exact location lost to time.

The story of the Lost Cabin Gold Mine dates back to the 19th century, during the height of the gold rush era. Prospectors from all corners of the nation flocked to the American West in search of fortune, and Wyoming, with its vast, untamed landscapes, was no exception.

The legend tells of a group of prospectors who stumbled upon an incredibly rich vein of gold in the Wind River Range. Excited by their find, they constructed a small cabin near the mine to serve as their base of operations. However, tragedy struck when a group of Native Americans, wary of the intruders on their land, attacked the prospectors, leaving none alive.

The location of the mine, known only to those now

deceased prospectors, became a tantalizing mystery, giving birth to the legend of the Lost Cabin Gold Mine.

Over the years, numerous adventurers and treasure hunters have attempted to uncover the lost mine, enticed by the prospect of unimaginable wealth waiting to be claimed. They scoured the Wind River Range, armed with scant clues and fueled by determination.

Despite these efforts, the Lost Cabin Gold Mine has remained elusive, its secrets closely guarded by the wilderness. Some have claimed to be close to discovery, while others have met with misfortune or tragedy, further adding to the legend's mystique.

As with many tales of lost treasures, the story of the Lost Cabin Gold Mine is met with a healthy dose of skepticism. Critics point out the lack of concrete evidence and argue that the tale is a product of folklore, embellished over generations.

Geologists and historians have also weighed in, suggesting that while gold is present in Wyoming, the likelihood of a secret, incredibly rich vein existing in the described manner is slim. They propose that the story could be a conflation of smaller, documented mining operations in the area.

Regardless of its veracity, the legend of the Lost Cabin Gold Mine has become an integral part of Wyoming's folklore. It has inspired books, articles, and expeditions, contributing to the state's rich tapestry of stories and mysteries.

The tale also serves as a reminder of the allure of the unknown and the human spirit's unyielding pursuit of adventure and discovery. It speaks to the enduring fascination with hidden treasures and the untamed wilderness that characterizes much of Wyoming's landscapes.

While some of these treasure stories have led to actual discoveries, others continue to fuel speculation, attracting treasure hunters and adventurers to the Continental Divide Trail in search of fortune and mystery. These tales serve as a testament to the enduring allure of the trail and the legends that continue to entwine with its history.

FEAR IN THE FOREST: VOLUME 1

CALLS FOR HELP

It was 2009 and I went camping with my boyfriend somewhere along the Appalachian Trail. I am still convinced that what we saw was absolute evil, in its purest form and I don't want to say exactly where we were because I don't want anyone to get any ideas about going there in search of this entity. I have always enjoyed being in the woods and that's one of the reasons my boyfriend and I meshed so well together. We met when we were both at the same two week long spiritual retreat and realized we had so much in common. The retreat went well and after six months of being together, I moved to the Midwest to be closer to him. I was born and raised in Maine but because I can work from anywhere and he can't, I decided to make the sacrifice of moving. It ended up working out and once I moved there he showed me a whole other part of the country and a whole different type of wilderness than anything that I was used to. We are also both very interested in the paranormal and love to take ghost tours all over the place. On this particular trip though we were just trying to unwind from a long week of work, from the stress of my move and just from everyday life as twenty-somethings just starting to make and find our own way in the world. The campsite he chose was spectacular and I knew right away it was going to be a great time.

We had one very large tent that we were sharing and he knew more about the outdoors than I did and that's saying something because I was basically raised in the wilderness. Family vacations were always spent camping, hiking or doing some other amazing activity outdoors and as a family. We built a fire, had some dinner and, after stargazing for about an hour, we decided to go into the tent and call it a night at around midnight. Aside from the fact that we saw what looked like several shooting stars, only they were bright, glowing green, there was nothing creepy or off putting about the forest up until that point. It was almost like the second we got into our tents and got settled in, we both felt like the energy of the whole place had just shifted somehow. We couldn't put our fingers on it at first but eventually we decided that, although we couldn't hear anything and there wasn't anything there that we could see, we felt like we were being watched by something right outside of our tent. It was terrifying because we had both been looking into encounters in the woods right before we left for this trip. We were planning on camping for a week but after that first night we decided to move and find somewhere else to set up our camp. We hardly got any sleep and it wasn't only because of the eerie feelings we both had when we finally laid down either. The entire night we kept being woken up by a child yelling and pleading for help. Of course, we grabbed our flashlights and went out into the woods to look for the little girl we were hearing but we never found anyone. It just gave us a bad feeling. I mean, why would there be a little girl yelling for help in the middle of the woods, out in the middle of nowhere in the middle of the night? It didn't make any sense. After the fourth time we didn't even bother to go and look anymore and honestly we both felt like something was trying to lure us deeper into the woods. I always look back on that night and on that trip and thank heavens that he and I both were very aware of not only the fact that paranormal entities oftentimes stalk wooded areas and especially forests, but that they will lure you to your death sometimes as well. Who knows what would have happened to us if we hadn't given up for the night? It depends on what you're dealing with and, honestly, whether or not you believe in it.

There weren't any other people camping in the area where we were, or at least we didn't see anyone and there shouldn't have been. The woods were very isolated and out of the way and so we didn't expect to see anyone. When we heard a little girl we knew something just wasn't right. We hardly slept and first thing the next morning we had some breakfast and then hiked two miles further into the woods in the hopes that we wouldn't have to deal with whatever was happening at the initial campsite. We weren't freaked out enough to give up on the trip and since the paranormal was kind of our thing, we were sort of exhilarated by the experience. Not enough to investigate, but enough that we thought it was gonna be a cool and creepy story to tell our friends. We hung out and hiked a bit and eventually it was time to go to bed again. All had been quiet up until that point and we hadn't seen or heard anyone else anywhere near us.

Sure enough though, as soon as we got into the tent that eerie and creepy feeling came over the both of us again and we somehow just knew that we hadn't heard the last of the little girl. We felt whatever it was, it was extremely negative, therefore we didn't try to record or photograph anything in any way. We hadn't seen it, yet, but I wish we had set up our cameras. We were equipped to have gotten the activity on video but we just felt like that would've caused us more trouble. We kissed goodnight and went to sleep hoping for the best but expecting to be woken up all night long again. We weren't wrong in having that expectation. Sure enough, right around two in the morning we heard a little girl crying. She wasn't yelling or screaming for help that time but she was moaning and crying like she was really sad. Of course this tugged at our heartstrings despite knowing what we were both feeling intuitively and also what we had obviously gone through the night before. We were considering leaving and calling the police. There was no cell service in that area anyway, even if we had cell phones, which we didn't at the time. After about fifteen minutes of incessant crying and moaning we had finally had enough and gave in. We grabbed our flashlights and went to look for the little girl. Neither of us expected to find a little girl but we had to look just in case there was one who needed help. It was highly unlikely I know but it's hard to explain how you react to something like this when you're in the moment.

We tried to follow the sound of where the cries seemed to be coming from. After about twenty minutes of randomly wandering the woods we were about to give up and go back to our tent. We had made the decision that the next day we were going to go into town and report it to the local authorities. Turns out we would have no reason to do any such thing. Suddenly the forest went silent and grew very still. The cries stopped as we stood directly in front of a really tall and wide tree. It was much taller than any of the others around it and the front of it looked like it had some sort of strange carvings or symbols on it. We hadn't remembered seeing it earlier in the night, despite it seeming like it would be really hard to miss, and we had circled back around to that area at least twice. There was grayish white fog starting to form around the tree and all over the place in the area where we were standing. It engulfed everything and it was suddenly very hard to see. He and I were both really scared right away because we knew this was not normal and the fog wasn't a natural phenomenon. I couldn't see my boyfriend but I could hear him and he told me to just stay still so we could think of how to get out of there without losing one another. I reached for his hand and he grabbed it, or so I thought. I heard him ask where I was and I told him I was "right here", meaning I was holding his hand. He asked me "right where" and that's when I told him I was holding his hand. He said I wasn't doing any such thing and that's when it hit me how far away he had sounded. I immediately tried to let go of who or whatever's hand I was holding but it clenched its hand around mine and squeezed. I screamed in pain and terror.

I looked over in that direction and I saw a creature next to me. I could somehow see it through the dense and very intense fog. It was about ten feet tall, white like the color of a crayon labeled as white, not caucasian or even just pale, and it had extremely large, black eyes. The eyes reminded me of a cat. They stared into mine and I felt myself start to get dizzy. I wanted to take in more of the creature before it led me to whatever fate it had in store for me. It had what looked like antennae on top of its head and there was a green light emanating from its whole body, all around it. Its fingers were long and spindly but they were circular at the end. Instead of having fingernails there seemed to only be circular little nubs at the tips. I kept trying to pull my hand away but its grip was too tight. I also noticed it had a nose and the shape of where the eyebrows went and formed the nose that also reminded me of a cat. Its mouth looked perfectly normal. I screamed and that must have been when I passed out. However, I didn't hit the ground because the entity wouldn't let go of my hand. It simply jerked my arm back up and I was once again standing normally and it had my full attention. I yelled for my boyfriend but got no response. The fog had lifted. I tried to look around to see if I could locate him but I also didn't want to take my eyes off of the being that had me by my hand and didn't seem to have any intentions on letting it go anytime soon. A bright blue light blasted out of the sky right in front of us. It almost blinded me and I used my other hand to shield my eyes. I looked over at the being and its mouth opened unusually wide and it reminded me of a snake who dislocates its jaw when about to or in the middle of devouring its prey. I screamed again but it just mimicked me and screamed my voice back at me. I was shaking and I stopped walking and stubbornly stood there. I was overwhelmed with and overcome by fear and complete and total panic. I didn't know what to do.

Suddenly and seemingly out of nowhere I was being pulled backwards by two strong arms around my waist. It was my boyfriend and he looked like he had been swimming or something because he was soaking wet. His brave attempt at freeing me had caught the creature off guard and it lost its grip on my hand. The light from the sky vanished, the remaining fog went with it and the creature turned to us and angrily howled. Then, as we watched, it floated right into the tree and disappeared. Within minutes we could hear the sounds of a little girl crying and calling out for help. We ran as fast as we could but we had no idea where our camp was. We were lured out there and didn't remember how far we had gone or which way we had come from. We ran and ran regardless and eventually we did make it back to our camp. We couldn't leave right then because it was the middle of the night and there were other, known predators out there that could attack and kill us. We had to wait it out. We got back in our tent and honestly, we didn't even talk about it. We were both so incredibly exhausted, probably from the extreme rushes of adrenaline, that we both just cuddled up and passed out. We woke up at ten the next morning. We got out of our tent intent on packing everything up immediately and hiking back out of there. However, we got out of the tent and realized we were right under that gigantic, strange tree where the entity had disappeared into. Our entire camp; our tent, all of our belongings, everything, had somehow been transported, while we slept, to that spot. We knew right then that something otherworldly had happened to us but we had no idea what. We just wanted to get the hell out of there and so we did.

We talked about it a little bit but my boyfriend, who is now my husband, wouldn't ever open up to me about where he had gone that night or why he came back soaking wet. It's too traumatic I guess and I hope that someday he will feel like he can tell me. We both believe wholeheartedly that we had been abducted and that it more than likely wasn't the first or the last time. We also are pretty sure we aren't the only ones. We are both considering hypnotic regression therapy but we aren't quite ready yet. Either together or individually, we are both still very fearful of what we might uncover. I put this out there in the hopes that other people who have experienced something similar, whether out in the woods, in that same area or otherwise, won't feel so alone and afraid. My boyfriend and I never discussed what happened to us with anyone other than each other. It just seems safer that way. I think my writing it all down is the first step to finding out more and being able to share our story with more people, all over the world. These things really do happen to regular people and we don't know why we were chosen, why at that time, in that place; we don't know anything at all except for our experiences. He doesn't know I'm sharing this but with all of the research he does he will more than likely come across it one day. I'm not sure how he will react but for me it's been very therapeutic and I thank you for letting me get it off my chest.

* * *

FEAR IN THE FOREST

Publisher's Excerpt 2

I SAW BIGFOOT

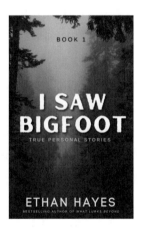

SOUTH CAROLINA SIGHTING

So, I'm not really sure about the exact order of things that happened, but let me know if you think this is weird or not. I never realized what one of these things were until I started listening to your podcast a few years ago. I emailed you a while back, but I didn't share all of my experiences that happened at my childhood home where my mom still lives.

So, I grew up in Marion, SC. It's a tiny town about an hour away from Myrtle Beach. Population's around 6 thousand, and it's spread out. Mom's still out there in the country. Back then, we had two houses on our right, and one across the road from us, opposite a few fields. Country life, you know? To the left and behind our place, there were just fields for miles. Depending on the season, it'd be corn, soybeans, or tobacco. I got two older sisters, and we all lived in this small home with a barn-like thing we called the boat shed. Dad kept his boats, lawnmower, and stuff like that there. In our backyard, we had this big oak tree, and this massive magnolia tree in the front. Funny thing is, mom actually grew up on that land and moved back after she got married and had us.

We used to have these "prowler" issues, as my parents would say. Banging on windows, things going missing from the boat shed, and these "people" peeking into our windows. Now, let me tell you about one time. I was probably around 10 years old, and I had this major fear of the dark – whole different story why – and my big sis asked if I could spend a night in her room. My other sis and I shared bunk beds in another room, and we were super tight, like best buds. Me and the older sis, we had our moments, you know? She could be real mean, but sometimes she'd surprise me with some kindness. Should've been suspicious, really. So, I thought it was cool she was asking me to crash in her room, even though I was kinda scared of her.

Anyway, her room was like pitch black, only light was this red glow from her digital clock on the dresser. So, there we are, in our PJs, and she's telling me to get into bed. This bed's shoved in a corner, so you can only get in from one side. I crawl in, heart already racing 'cause I'm thinking, "What's she up to?" She's being weirdly nice, saying not to be scared, that she'll hold my hand till I fall asleep. I'm thinking she's planning something, like smothering me or something, LOL. So, we're lying there, it's a decently comfy bed, and she kills the light. I'm lying there, feeling better 'cause I can see a bit from the light coming through the blinds. She's like, "It's all good, I'm right here." I'm like, "Fine, whatever." I'm not sure why she's acting so chill, but it's late, and my eyes are getting used to the dark and the tiny bit of light.

I start drifting off, not sure how long I was out, but suddenly, I hear tapping. Even as I type this now, I'm feeling exactly how I felt that night, like 40 years later! I'm just looking around with my eyes, frozen with fear. I don't know why I'm so scared, 'cause I don't know what the sound is. I move my arm under the covers to feel if my sister's there, and yep, she's there, fast asleep. The tapping's coming from the window and it's getting louder and louder. I shift my eyes over, not moving my head, and I see this HUGE dark figure blocking most of the window. I'm holding my breath, feet freezing, realizing that's fear, right? I'm petrified. I think these "prowlers" are trying to break in. The blinds are kinda slanted down, so lying there, I can see a bit of whatever it is. All I can make out is that it's black and has these super white teeth. A big ol' mouthful of 'em, and I can hear it breathing, all raspy and gurgly.

I grab my sister's arm, whisper-shout, "Someone's at the window." She's like, "What?" I say, "Someone's trying to get in!" Trying not to move, talking real low. She shouts, "What?" I scream, "Someone's trying to get in!" She looks, sees the figure, and bolts out of the room, screaming for Dad. I slide out of bed, don't look back 'til I hit the floor, then crawl outta there faster than lightning. "Dad, Dad, someone's trying to get in the window! Hurry!" Now, Mom and Dad are asleep, but Dad jumps up when we scream, grabs his .38 revolver – yeah, he had that thing for dealing with these "prowlers" – and dashes out the front door in his underwear. Mom calls the neighbors, they grab their guns too and go help Dad. Mom's convinced they're gonna accidentally shoot each other, but that's Dad. He comes back in a bit, saying he heard 'em running through the tobacco field, saw a dark figure breaking the stalks, but couldn't see details. And just like that, we're supposed to go back to bed like it's all normal. Yeah, right. I'm in the living room, sis goes back to bed, parents too.

I'm glued to the TV the whole dang night, totally freaked. I can still see it now, like I'm there. Can still hear it. Do I know what that thing was? Nope. But listening to your episodes where people talk about hooded folks or mysterious figures, it all comes rushing back. So, about a year ago, I went back to Mom's. Listened to some more of your guests' stories, talked to Mom – Dad's gone, passed away six years back – but Mom's still holding strong at 84, got my nephew with her, so she's not alone. She's got a load of stories from that house, which I'll share someday. Went back to that window where that "person" was ages ago, measured it up. No bricks or flower beds under there, just the hedges that were always there. The window's bottom is at 5 feet, and that thing took up the whole dang window!

So, I'm guessing it was like 7 and a half, maybe 8 feet tall, unless whoever it was had a ladder or something. Me and Mom just stood there, totally amazed. How did we just think that was a regular person? It hit me like a ton of bricks! Told a few close friends, got the "You're crazy" look and a grin, so I let it be. But I can't. The more I think about all the wild stuff that happened out there, something was going on, man.

* * *

I SAW BIGFOOT: BOOK 1

Eight

DANGERS ON THE TRAIL

HIKING the Continental Divide Trail (CDT) poses a unique set of challenges for adventurers. The high elevations can lead to altitude sickness, while the vast range in altitudes exposes hikers to both cold temperatures at higher elevations and intense heat in the lower sections. The Rockies are known for their sudden storms, with a particular risk of lightning strikes. The trail itself presents rugged paths with steep inclines and rocky surfaces, and some river crossings with swift currents can be treacherous. Hikers should also be cautious of wildlife encounters, including bears, mountain lions, and moose. Navigation can be a challenge as the CDT isn't always well-marked, increasing the risk of getting lost. Additionally, the trail's remote sections mean that help can be delayed in emergencies, and certain stretches pose the challenge of water scarcity due to limited sources.

The Last Trek of Stephen "Otter" Olshansky

The world of long-distance hiking is populated by individuals who seek to conquer the unyielding expanses of nature, propelled by passion, determination, and the allure of adventure. Stephen "Otter" Olshansky was one such individual, with dreams as expansive as the trails he traversed. But as every hiker knows, with dreams come the inevitable risks that test one's limits.

Stephen Olshansky was no stranger to the world of long-distance hiking. By 2015, he had successfully navigated two of the major U.S. trails – the Pacific Crest Trail and the Appalachian Trail. These achievements weren't just hikes; they were milestones in a journey that spans thousands of miles, each step weaving a story of triumphs, challenges, friendships, and solitude.

The Continental Divide Trail (CDT) beckoned as the final leg of what hikers reverently call the "Triple Crown." Spanning from Mexico to Canada, the CDT winds its way along the Rocky Mountains, presenting a unique set of challenges and terrains.

Starting his journey on the CDT in early 2015, Olshansky had all the markings of a seasoned hiker. With a trail name like "Otter," he had a certain fluidity and ease with which he approached the wilderness. But even the most experienced cannot predict the whims of nature.

As Olshansky trekked into New Mexico in November, a blanket of early winter settled in. These conditions, unusual and harsh for the season, hampered his progress, layering his journey with treacherous snow and plummeting temperatures. The trail that once held the promise of discovery now posed significant dangers.

By the time Olshansky reached the Gila National Forest's vicinity, his communications with family and friends became less frequent, then ceased. Alarm bells rang within the tight-knit community of hikers and his concerned family. With each passing day, the hope of finding Otter safe dwindled, replaced by a growing dread.

A search operation ensued, driven by a collective effort from fellow hikers, local communities, and authorities. Yet, the vast expanse of the Gila, coupled with the thick blanket of snow, obscured any trace of Otter's path.

It wasn't until February 2016, after the snow began to recede, that searchers stumbled upon a tragic scene. Olshansky's remains lay near the trail, offering a silent testament to his struggle against nature's elements. The exact circumstances of his death remain clouded in mystery, but the severe winter conditions were undeniably a major factor.

The news of Stephen "Otter" Olshansky's death sent ripples across the hiking community. While his story stands as a somber reminder of the unpredictability of nature and the risks of solo hiking, it also illuminates the spirit of the hiking community – bound by mutual respect, concern, and an unwavering love for the trail.

Olshansky's legacy is not just one of caution but of inspiration. He epitomized the spirit of adventure and the pursuit of dreams, no matter the challenges. In the silent whispers of the wind across the trail, in the rustling of the leaves, and in the footprints on the path, Stephen "Otter" Olshansky's story lives on, inspiring and cautioning generations of hikers to come.

* * *

The Mysterious Disappearance of Joe Keller:

In 2015, Joe Keller, a 19-year-old athlete and adventurer, disappeared without a trace, leaving behind a trail of unanswered questions and a community in shock.

Joe, an enthusiastic runner and nature lover, was on a road trip with a friend, venturing through the picturesque landscapes of Colorado. On July 23, they decided to make a stop at the Rainbow Trout Ranch in Conejos County, near the Colorado-New Mexico border. The ranch, renowned for its stunning vistas and tranquil setting, seemed like the perfect place for Joe to indulge his passion for outdoor activities.

In the late afternoon, Joe set out for a run, a routine activity for the athletic young man. Dressed in a black tank top, black shorts, and red running shoes, he headed towards the Forest Road 250, adjacent to the ranch, planning to explore the area and get a good workout. His friends expected him to return in an hour, as he was a fast and experienced runner.

However, as the sun dipped below the horizon, casting long shadows across the landscape, there was no sign of Joe. Panic began to set in, and his friends alerted the authorities, initiating a search and rescue operation that would span several days.

The search for Joe Keller was extensive and grueling. Over 200 personnel, including search and rescue teams, law enforcement, and volunteers, scoured the rugged terrain, hoping to find any clue that might lead them to the missing young man. Helicopters and search dogs were deployed, and the community rallied together, united in their determination to bring Joe home.

Yet, despite their tireless efforts, the search yielded no results. Joe had vanished, leaving behind a mystery that baffled investigators and haunted his family and friends. The terrain, with its dense forests, steep inclines, and hidden crevices, proved to be a formidable adversary, concealing Joe's whereabouts from those desperately seeking answers.

As days turned into weeks, and weeks into months, the active search for Joe was eventually called off. The Keller family, devastated but not defeated, continued their own efforts to find Joe, offering rewards for information and working with private investigators to uncover any leads.

In 2016, nearly a year after Joe's disappearance, a hiker stumbled upon human remains in the vicinity of the search area. Forensic analysis confirmed that they belonged to Joe Keller. The discovery brought a tragic end to the long search, but it also raised new questions. The cause of Joe's death remained undetermined, and the circumstances surrounding his disappearance were as mysterious as ever.

Joe's case has since become a haunting chapter in the history of the Rocky Mountains and the Continental Divide Trail. His disappearance serves as a stark reminder of the unpredictability of nature and the inherent risks of venturing into remote wilderness areas. The mystery of what happened to Joe Keller on that fateful day remains unsolved, leaving a lingering sense of unease and speculation in its wake.

Beware of the wildlife:

On July 22, 2023, Amie Adamson, 48, was tragically killed while she had been running or hiking alone on a forest trail approximately 8 miles west of Yellowstone National Park. Officials had reported that the bear, accompanied by one or more cubs, had likely attacked Adamson during an unforeseen encounter before vacating the area. Montana Fish, Wildlife and Parks officials had posited that the bear's actions had been defensive, a behavior typical for grizzly bears. The exact sequence of events remained unclear due to the lack of witnesses and the bear not being found.

In the days that followed her death, efforts to locate the bear had included setting traps made from metal culverts, baited with meat around the scene of the incident. However, these attempts over three nights hadn't been successful. Game wardens had then decided to keep a watch over the area for another week. For safety, the national forest lands around the incident location had been closed, with a planned reopening on August 25, pending further decisions.

Adamson, who was originally from Kansas and had been a teacher, had shifted her focus from education, choosing instead to backpack across parts of the U.S. She had also penned a book detailing her journeys. Her family had shared that she held a deep passion for her outdoor activities, and she had made it a daily routine to walk, hike, or run every morning.

The unfortunate incident had occurred on a trail that was popular among hikers, horseback riders, and off-road vehicle enthusiasts, situated about 8 miles from West Yellowstone, a primary access point to the national park. Notably, Adamson hadn't carried bear spray, a tool often recommended in areas known for grizzly bear activity. Her body had been found by another hiker at around 8 a.m. that fateful Saturday. The coroner's office later confirmed that her death had resulted from excessive blood loss due to a bear attack.

At the site, investigators had identified tracks indicative of a grizzly and at least one cub. A trail camera had also managed to capture an image of a grizzly bear accompanied by two cubs in the vicinity that Saturday night. Despite this evidence, there had been no further sightings or encounters reported.

* * *

The Continental Divide Trail (CDT) offers a breathtaking wilderness experience, but it also comes with inherent risks. From unpredictable weather and challenging terrains to potential encounters with wildlife, hikers must be well-prepared and vigilant to ensure their safety while traversing this iconic trail.

Nine

MYSTERIOUS CREATURES

While there are numerous legends, folktales, and mythological accounts associated with the regions that the Continental Divide Trail (CDT) traverses, there aren't a lot of well-documented true encounters with "mysterious creatures" on the CDT.

* * *

Bigfoot (Sasquatch):

The most famous cryptid in North America, Bigfoot stories are pervasive throughout the continent. The Rocky Mountains, which the CDT traverses, is no exception. There have been numerous Bigfoot sightings in the Rockies, with individuals reporting large footprints, unidentified vocalizations, and even direct encounters with a tall, hairy, bipedal creature.

The name "Sasquatch" is an Anglicized derivative of the word "Sésquac," which means "wild man" in a Salish Native American language. Long before Europeans set foot on North American soil, indigenous tribes from California to the Pacific Northwest had tales of large, hairy, bipedal creatures that lived deep in the woods. These creatures were, in many stories, seen as spirits or protectors of the woods, possessing supernatural abilities to blend into their surroundings or vanish into thin air.

The modern fascination with Bigfoot began mainly in the mid-20th century, especially after a series of footprint casts were discovered in California in the 1950s. Since then, sightings have been reported across North America, from the swamps of Florida to the snowy peaks of the Rocky Mountains. But the dense forests of the Pacific Northwest, including those the PCT traverses, remain a significant hotspot for Bigfoot reports.

Those who claim to have seen Bigfoot often describe it as standing between 7 to 10 feet tall, covered in dark brown or reddish hair, and having a distinctive foul odor. Its eyes, when caught in the beam of a flashlight or lantern, are said to glow red or yellow. Contrary to the menacing portrayal in some media, many reports suggest Bigfoot is more curious than aggressive, often watching from a distance or trying to avoid human interaction.

-Encounter:

I was dead set on reaching the summit of Mt. Elbert, the highest peak in Colorado. I had already tried twice before, but both times I had to turn back due to bad weather. Determined as ever, I decided to go solo this time around. It was late June of 2009 and I set out from the trailhead early in the morning all by myself.

The weather that day was surprisingly perfect and warm for the season. It seemed like there hadn't been much snow during the winter because even at the summit, there was very little snow left. I reached the top at around 1:45 pm, basking in the accomplishment. The view was breathtaking, and I took some pictures with my trusty digital camera to capture the moment.

However, it wasn't until later, around 3:30 pm and at an altitude of approximately 11,500 feet, that something truly extraordinary happened. I was making my way down, feeling exhausted from the long hike. The trail I was on wasn't very popular due to its steepness and ruggedness, so I hadn't encountered a single person all day. As I traversed through the only level portion of the trail, a high mountain plateau that lasted for about 300 yards, I heard a strange sound—a mix between a scream and a growl, with a surprisingly high pitch. The sound seemed to carry for miles, sending shivers down my spine.

I immediately froze in my tracks, my hand instinctively reaching for the holster of my pistol. I scanned the area, trying to locate the source of the sound, but the mountainous terrain made it difficult to pinpoint. I first looked to my right, into the dense pine forest, but I couldn't spot anything unusual. Slowly, I did a full 360-degree scan, and that's when I saw it—a Bigfoot, standing about 7 to 7 1/2 feet tall, approximately 50 yards away from me. I was wearing army camo, and for a few seconds, I could tell the creature was trying to figure me out. I was both terrified and amazed, so I couldn't bring myself to move.

Suddenly, the Bigfoot turned around and took off with incredible speed and long strides. It ran in a way that resembled a human's movement, albeit with a slightly hunched upper back and a more powerful gait. Its fur or hair appeared to be a mix of black and brown, thick and matted in certain areas. I lost sight of it after about 10 seconds of its rapid retreat. At that point, my heart was pounding so hard that I thought it might burst out of my chest. The sound of my own heartbeat echoed in my ears. Without hesitation, I pulled out my pistol and cautiously continued down the trail, filled with adrenaline. I constantly looked over my shoulder, scanning my surroundings, not taking any chances.

It wasn't until I reached the cabin I had rented that I realized my camera had been in my backpack the whole time. I hadn't even thought about capturing the incredible sighting on film. But that didn't matter to me in the end. I knew what I had seen, and no one could ever take that away from me.

To this day, the memory of that encounter is etched deeply in my mind. It was a surreal experience, one that I will always carry with me, reminding me of the mysteries that lie within the unexplored corners of our world.

Skinwalkers:

Primarily associated with Navajo folklore, skinwalkers are said to be witches who can transform into animals. While the core of skinwalker stories is more associated with areas in Arizona, Utah, and New Mexico, some portions of the CDT in New Mexico might have tales or legends related to these beings.

Skinwalkers, or "yee naaldlooshii" in the Navajo language, translate to "with it, he goes on all fours." This term is deeply rooted in Navajo culture, representing a type of witch or malevolent sorcerer who has gained the power to transform into, possess, or disguise themselves as animals. Skinwalkers are often depicted as coyotes, wolves, foxes, eagles, owls, or crows. These beings are feared and respected, believed to possess the ability to curse and harm those they target.

Skinwalker tales are most prevalent in the Southwest, particularly in areas close to Navajo reservations. The CDT crosses through New Mexico, which is rich in Native American history and folklore, making it a region where tales of Skinwalkers might be more prevalent. It is important to note that discussions about Skinwalkers are often taboo within Native American communities. The topic is usually avoided, and the stories are not shared lightly, adding an aura of mystery and secrecy to the lore.

While there aren't well-documented encounters of Skinwalkers specifically on the CDT, the trail's proximity to regions where these tales originate has led to whispers and rumors among hikers. Tales of eerie noises, unexplained animal sightings, and a general feeling of unease in certain sections of the trail contribute to the atmosphere of mystery.

Skeptics argue that tales of Skinwalkers, like many folklore stories, are ways to explain the unexplainable, instill social order, or provide moral lessons. The isolation and vastness of the CDT, combined with the physical and mental challenges of long-distance hiking, can lead to heightened senses and a propensity to interpret natural phenomena as something more mysterious.

While there is no concrete evidence to support the existence of Skinwalkers along the CDT, the tales add a layer of cultural richness and mystery to the trail experience. They remind us of the deep connection between the land and its original inhabitants, as well as the power of stories to evoke fear, wonder, and respect for the unknown elements of the wilderness. Whether one believes in Skinwalkers or not, the tales are an integral part of the folklore surrounding the Continental Divide Trail, showcasing the intersection of nature, culture, and mystery.

Thunderbirds:

The Thunderbird, a mythical creature deeply rooted in Native American folklore, is described as an enormous bird, capable of creating storms and thunder with the flap of its wings. Stories of these formidable birds have been passed down through generations, with various tribes attributing different characteristics and significance to the creature.

As hikers traverse the CDT, they find themselves immersed in the landscapes that have fueled these legends for centuries. The high altitudes and isolated terrain provide a fitting backdrop for the tales of the Thunderbird, creating an aura of mystery that envelops the trail.

While there is no scientific evidence to support the existence of Thunderbirds, sightings and stories continue to circulate, capturing the imaginations of hikers, locals, and enthusiasts alike. Descriptions of the creature vary, with some recounting seeing giant birds with wingspans of up to 20 feet, while others describe more mystical features, suggesting a creature that transcends the boundaries of the natural world.

Skeptics attribute these sightings to misidentifications of large birds such as eagles or condors, or to the tricks that isolation and the elements can play on the mind. However, for believers, the Thunderbird represents something more —a connection to the past, a symbol of the untamed spirit of the wilderness, and a reminder of the mysteries that still linger in the remote corners of the world.

As hikers venture along the CDT, the legend of the Thunderbird serves as a poignant reminder of the rich tapestry of stories and beliefs that have been woven into the landscape. It challenges them to look beyond the visible terrain and contemplate the unseen, the unexplained, and the extraordinary.

Whether regarded as a mere myth or embraced as a symbol of the wilderness and its enduring mysteries, the

Thunderbird remains a fascinating aspect of the lore surrounding the Continental Divide Trail. It captures the essence of the trail itself—a journey through the unknown, a challenge to the spirit, and an adventure that leaves an indelible mark on all who traverse it.

El Chupacabra:

The Chupacabra, a creature of Latin American folklore, has fascinated and terrified people for decades. Descriptions of the creature vary, but it is often depicted as a reptilian creature with spines or quills running down its back, capable of leaping like a kangaroo, and with a taste for the blood of livestock. The legend of the Chupacabra has traveled far and wide, sparking curiosity, skepticism, and fear.

The Chupacabra is said to have originated in Puerto Rico in the 1990s, with the first reported attacks on livestock occurring in the town of Moca. The name "Chupacabra" itself translates to "goat-sucker" in Spanish, referring to the creature's supposed habit of drinking the blood of domestic animals. From Puerto Rico, reports of Chupacabra sightings spread to Mexico, the U.S., and other parts of Latin America.

Wildlife biologists and experts have often attributed Chupacabra sightings to misidentifications of known animals, particularly in states of disease or decay. Canids with mange, for instance, can exhibit a grotesque appearance that might be mistaken for a Chupacabra. Along the CDT, diverse wildlife is present, and it's possible that hikers or locals could misidentify an animal, especially under the influence of the region's many legends and tales.

Scientists and skeptics have extensively studied the Chupacabra phenomenon, often concluding that the creature is a result of mass hysteria, misidentification, and the power of urban legends. Along the CDT, as in many other parts of the world, these rational explanations are often less exciting than the allure of the mysterious and unknown.

While the Chupacabra is a captivating element of Latin American folklore, its connections to the CDT are tenuous at best. The trail offers a rich tapestry of history, culture, and natural beauty, but the Chupacabra remains a creature of myth, its stories more likely to be found in the communities along the trail than in the wilderness of the CDT itself.

Dogman:

The Dogman, described as a humanoid creature with canine features, is a legend that predates the establishment of the CDT. Originating from Native American folklore and later embraced in local tales across the United States, the Dogman is said to be a creature that walks on two legs, has the head of a wolf or dog, and possesses a towering and intimidating stature.

While there have been sporadic reports of Dogman sightings in various parts of North America, the creature's association with the CDT is less prominent compared to other cryptids. However, the vastness and remoteness of the trail provide a fertile ground for the imagination, and tales of eerie encounters and strange noises in the woods have surfaced over the years.

Hikers and locals alike have occasionally reported feeling a sense of being watched, hearing unexplained growls or howls, and finding large, unusual tracks. These accounts are often shared around campfires, contributing to the lore of the trail and sparking debates on the existence of such cryptic entities.

As with many cryptid stories, accounts of the Dogman are met with skepticism. Biologists and wildlife experts argue that the sightings could be misidentified known animals, such as bears, wolves, or coyotes. The play of shadows in the woods, coupled with the solitude of the trail, can also play tricks on the human mind, leading to exaggerated or imagined encounters.

Regardless of one's stance on the existence of the Dogman, the creature has undeniably become a part of the folklore surrounding the Continental Divide Trail. The tales add an element of mystery and allure to the trail, capturing the imaginations of hikers, storytellers, and cryptozoology enthusiasts alike.

In the realm of folklore and legend, the Dogman stands as a testament to humanity's fascination with the unknown and the eerie. As hikers traverse the CDT, the stories of the Dogman live on, passed down through generations and shared amongst the whispers of the pines and the shadows of the mountains.

The stories of mysterious creatures along the CDT remind us that, in the heart of the wilderness, there is always room for the unknown and the unexplained. These tales challenge our perceptions and invite us to question what lies beyond the realm of the known. They encourage us to embrace the unknown and to respect the wilderness not just as a physical space, but as a realm filled with stories, history, and mysteries yet to be unraveled.

Ten

WEMINUCHE WILDERNESS MYSTERIES

IN THE HEART of the Colorado Rockies, the Weminuche Wilderness stands as the largest wilderness area in the state, encompassing a sprawling 499,771 acres of rugged terrain, dense forests, and towering peaks. With the Continental Divide Trail (CDT) weaving through its expanse, the Weminuche Wilderness has long captivated the imaginations of hikers, adventurers, and those drawn to the unknown. Amidst its undeniable beauty, the area has also been a source of mystery and intrigue, with tales of strange phenomena, unexplained events, and eerie sensations reported by those who have ventured into its depths.

The Weminuche Wilderness is characterized by its challenging terrain, diverse ecosystems, and remote nature. Its landscape is a mosaic of alpine meadows, dense forests, and high mountain peaks, including the impressive 14,093-foot Mount Eolus. This isolation and wildness have made the area a hotbed for legends and stories, as the vastness of the wilderness leaves ample room for the imagination to roam.

-Strange Lights and Unearthly Glows:

One of the most commonly reported mysteries in the Weminuche Wilderness is the appearance of strange lights and unearthly glows. Hikers and campers have recounted seeing mysterious illuminations in the night sky or amongst the trees, often described as orbs or glowing phenomena that seem to move with intelligence. While some of these sightings could be attributed to natural occurrences such as bioluminescent organisms or atmospheric conditions, not all have found conclusive explanations.

-Eerie Sounds and Whispering Winds:

The wilderness is also known for its eerie sounds that

permeate the night. Reports of unexplained noises, from distant howls and cries to strange rustlings in the underbrush, have been a staple of campfire tales. Skeptics argue that these sounds could be the calls of wildlife or the result of natural acoustics in the mountainous terrain. Yet, some who have experienced them insist that there is something more, something unworldly about these nocturnal symphonies.

-Feelings of Unease and Disorientation:

Many visitors to the Weminuche Wilderness describe a pervasive feeling of being watched or a sense of unease that descends upon them, especially in certain areas or during specific times of day. Some have reported sudden disorientation or a feeling of being lost, even when well within their navigational bearings. While these experiences could be chalked up to the psychological effects of solitude and the wilderness, they contribute to the area's reputation as a place of mystery.

-Historical Anomalies and Lost Treasures:

The Weminuche Wilderness has its share of historical mysteries as well. There are tales of lost mines and hidden treasures dating back to the days of the gold rush, with prospectors who vanished into the wilderness, leaving behind tantalizing clues. Additionally, the region's Native American heritage contributes ancient legends and stories, adding a layer of cultural mystique.

-The Role of the Environment:

Environmental factors play a significant role in many of the Weminuche Wilderness's mysteries. The high altitudes, challenging weather conditions, and isolation can impact a person's physical and mental state, potentially leading to hallucinations or heightened sensitivity to the surroundings. Biologists and naturalists also point to the diverse and sometimes elusive wildlife in the area as potential sources for some of the strange sightings and sounds.

As the sun sets over the rugged peaks of the Weminuche Wilderness, the shadows lengthen, and the mysteries deepen. This vast and wild expanse of Colorado remains a place of intrigue, where the line between the known and the unknown blurs, and the whispers of the wilderness beckon to those daring enough to seek answers. Whether these mysteries are the product of natural phenomena, the remnants of history, or something truly unexplained, they underscore the wilderness's allure and ensure that the Weminuche remains a place of wonder and enigma for generations to come.

Eleven

THE GHOSTS OF BANNACK, MONTANA

NESTLED in the rugged terrains of Montana, the ghost town of Bannack stands as a silent witness to a bygone era. Founded in 1862 following a significant gold discovery by John White and his party, Bannack quickly burgeoned into a bustling town, at one point even serving as the first territorial capital of Montana. Today, Bannack is preserved as a State Park, its remaining structures providing a haunting glimpse into the past.

The discovery of gold in Grasshopper Creek set off a rush to Bannack, drawing prospectors, adventurers, and entrepreneurs alike. The town's population soared, and Bannack became a center of opportunity and ambition. However, as with many mining towns of the era, the boom was short-lived. By the late 19th century, as the gold veins dwindled, Bannack's population declined, eventually leading to its abandonment.

Recognizing the historical significance of Bannack, the site was declared a State Park in 1954. Today, over sixty structures remain, ranging from the old hotel to the gallows, preserved in a state of arrested decay. Visitors can explore these remnants of the past, walking the same streets once trodden by miners, merchants, and outlaws.

As with many ghost towns, tales of the supernatural have woven themselves into the fabric of Bannack's history. Visitors and park rangers alike have reported various paranormal activities, contributing to the town's reputation as one of Montana's most haunted locations.

Numerous accounts of ghostly figures, shadowy apparitions, and unexplained phenomena have been reported in Bannack. The old hotel is said to be home to the spirit of a woman named Dorothy, who tragically drowned nearby. Visitors have reported seeing her image in the hotel's windows and hearing the rustle of her dress.

The gallows, where several outlaws met their end, is another hotspot of reported paranormal activity. Some claim to have captured orbs and strange light anomalies in photographs taken at the site.

The Ghost of Henry Plummer

One of Bannack's most infamous residents was Henry Plummer, a sheriff who was later revealed to be the leader of a notorious outlaw gang. Accused of orchestrating robberies and murders, Plummer was hanged by vigilantes in 1864. Some believe that his spirit lingers in Bannack, seeking redemption or perhaps vengeance.

Henry Plummer, whose spectral presence is believed by some to linger in Bannack, Montana, is a figure shrouded in mystery and controversy. Born in 1832, Plummer's life was a tumultuous journey that saw him rise to the position of sheriff, only to fall from grace amidst accusations of criminal conduct. His story is a compelling blend of fact and folklore, contributing significantly to Bannack's haunted reputation.

Henry Plummer arrived in Bannack in 1862, during the height of the gold rush. A charismatic and seemingly upstanding individual, he quickly ingratiated himself with the local community. In 1863, he was elected sheriff of Bannack and nearby Virginia City, a position that afforded him significant power and influence.

Despite his role as a lawman, rumors began to circulate that Plummer was leading a double life as the head of a notorious outlaw gang known as the "Innocents." This band of robbers and murderers was responsible for a spate of violent crimes, including robberies and killings, along the trails used by travelers and miners transporting gold.

Fed up with the lawlessness and convinced of Plummer's guilt, a group of vigilantes took matters into their own hands. In January 1864, they arrested Plummer along with several of his alleged accomplices. After a swift, informal trial, Henry Plummer was hanged on the gallows in Bannack – a structure that still stands today and is a focal point for ghostly tales.

The ghost of Henry Plummer is said to haunt Bannack, his spirit restless due to the controversial and violent nature of his death. Some believe that he lingers to clear his name, while others think he is seeking revenge against those who wronged him.

Visitors to Bannack have reported various paranormal occurrences that they attribute to the spirit of Henry Plummer. These reports include sightings of a shadowy figure near the gallows, unexplained sounds, and eerie feelings of being watched. Paranormal investigators who have visited the site claim to have captured evidence of ghostly activity, further fueling the legend of Henry Plummer's ghost.

The question of Henry Plummer's guilt or innocence remains a topic of debate among historians, researchers, and locals. Some believe that he was indeed the mastermind behind the "Innocents" and deserved his fate. Others argue that Plummer was a victim of vigilante justice and that he was wrongly accused.

Regardless of his guilt or innocence, the legend of Henry Plummer is an integral part of Bannack's history and allure. His story adds a layer of intrigue and mystery to the town, captivating the imaginations of those who visit and ponder the shadows of the past. The ghost of Henry Plummer, whether real or imagined, serves as a timeless reminder of Bannack's turbulent history and the thin line between legend and reality.

Through the years, the story of Henry Plummer has become an indelible part of Montana's folklore, ensuring that his presence is felt long after the final chapter of Bannack's history has been written.

While the ghost stories of Bannack captivate the imagination, they are met with skepticism by some. Critics argue that the tales are embellished or born from the eerie atmosphere of the abandoned town. Despite this, paranormal enthusiasts and curious visitors continue to flock to Bannack, eager to experience its mysteries firsthand.

Today, Bannack stands as a monument to the past, its silent streets and weathered structures telling the story of a time of tumult and transformation. The ghostly tales that linger in its air add a layer of mystery and intrigue, inviting visitors to ponder the thin line between history and legend. Whether one believes in the spectral inhabitants or not, the ghosts of Bannack serve as a poignant reminder that, in some places, the past is never truly gone.

Twelve

UTE LEGENDS

THE UTE PEOPLE, native to the Great Basin and the Rocky Mountain regions, have had a long and profound connection with the lands now known as Colorado, Utah, and New Mexico. With a history dating back to at least the 13th century, the Ute tribes have woven a rich tapestry of legends, rituals, and cultural practices centered around the majestic Rockies. The mountains, with their towering peaks, deep valleys, and vast expanses, have been both a home and a sacred space for the Ute, serving as a backdrop to their way of life and spiritual beliefs.

In Ute cosmology, the Rocky Mountains are not just a geographical feature; they are a living, spiritual entity, teeming with power and energy. This is a place where the earthly and spiritual realms intertwine, where ancestors dwell, and where the divine manifests itself. The Ute people practice animism, believing that everything in nature has a spirit, from the smallest pebble to the tallest mountain peak.

One of the most venerable Ute traditions is the Bear Dance, a ceremony steeped in legend and rich in symbolic meaning. The dance is held in the spring, coinciding with the bear's emergence from hibernation. According to Ute folklore, the dance was taught to the people by the bears themselves, as a way to strengthen the bonds between humans and the natural world. The ceremony involves a series of intricate steps and movements, accompanied by the rhythmic sound of the morache, a unique instrument made from the leaves of the box elder tree. The Bear Dance is a communal event, fostering social bonds and ensuring the community's spiritual wellbeing.

The Ute legends are filled with references to animal spirits, each serving as a guardian of the wilderness and a guide for human behavior. The bear, as mentioned earlier, is a symbol of strength, healing, and wisdom. The eagle represents clarity of vision and spiritual ascension, while the deer embodies gentleness and the importance of living in harmony with nature. These animal spirits are not just characters in stories; they are revered as real presences in the wilderness, guiding and protecting the Ute people.

The coyote holds a special place in Ute folklore as a trickster, a shape-shifter, and a master of disguise. The tales of the coyote are complex, often humorous, and always filled with lessons about the consequences of arrogance, the importance of cleverness, and the value of laughter. The coyote serves as a reminder that life is unpredictable, and wisdom often comes from unexpected places.

The Rocky Mountains are dotted with sites considered sacred by the Ute people. Peaks such as Pikes Peak in Colorado and Blanca Peak in the Sangre de Cristo Range are believed to be the homes of powerful spirits, and they have been destinations for pilgrimages and spiritual journeys for centuries. Hidden valleys, secluded springs, and ancient rock formations are all integral parts of the Ute spiritual landscape, serving as places of prayer, meditation, and connection to the divine.

As the modern world encroaches upon these ancient territories, the Ute people face the challenge of preserving their heritage and maintaining the sanctity of their sacred sites. Land rights, access to spiritual sites, and the preservation of cultural practices are ongoing issues, as the Ute work to protect their traditions for future generations.

The Continental Divide Trail, which winds its way through the heart of the Rockies, serves as a modern-day conduit through this storied landscape. Hikers who traverse the trail are immersed in the spiritual ambiance of the mountains, enveloped by the energy and mystery of the Ute legends. The stories of animal spirits, sacred rituals, and divine landscapes serve as a living testament to the enduring connection between the Ute people and the Rockies, a connection that continues to inspire, mystify, and captivate all who journey through this ancient and sacred terrain.

Thirteen

THE GHOSTS OF CHAMA, NEW MEXICO

NESTLED in the high country of Northern New Mexico, the small town of Chama serves as a pivotal waypoint for adventurers traversing the Continental Divide Trail (CDT). With its rich history, charming architecture, and breathtaking natural beauty, Chama also harbors tales from the past, whispering stories of the spectral and the mysterious. This chapter delves into the facts and the folklore surrounding the Ghosts of Chama, exploring the layers of history that have given rise to these enduring tales.

Founded in the late 19th century, Chama rapidly grew as a hub for the Denver and Rio Grande Western Railroad. The railroad brought prosperity, but it also bore witness to the struggles, triumphs, and tragedies of the era. The town's history is steeped in the legacy of the Old West, complete with stories of outlaws, hardworking pioneers, and moments of unexpected violence.

* * *

Foster's Hotel: A Haunted Landmark

One of the most storied buildings in Chama is Foster's Hotel, a historic structure that dates back to the town's heyday. Over the years, numerous guests and employees have reported eerie encounters within its walls.

-**The Woman in White**: Perhaps the most famous ghostly resident of Foster's Hotel is the Woman in White. Described as a spectral figure clad in a flowing white dress, she has been seen wandering the halls, her presence accompanied by a palpable sense of melancholy.

-**Unexplained Noises**: Guests have reported hearing footsteps in empty corridors, soft whispers in the dead of night, and the creaking of floorboards as if someone unseen is moving about.

The Railroad and Its Phantom Trains

The Denver and Rio Grande Western Railroad was the lifeblood of Chama, and it, too, has its share of ghostly lore.

-**Echos of the Past**: Residents and visitors have claimed to hear the distant sounds of train whistles and chugging locomotives, long after the last train has passed. These auditory phantoms serve as a reminder of the town's bustling past.

The Spirits of the Old West

Chama's ghosts are not confined to buildings or the remnants of the railroad; they are woven into the very fabric of the town.

-**Restless Outlaws**: Tales persist of spectral figures clad in cowboy attire, seen wandering near the old rail yards or along deserted streets, perhaps echoes of outlaws or townspeople from a bygone era.

-**Mysterious Lights**: There have been sightings of

unexplained lights in and around Chama, with various interpretations ranging from the paranormal to the natural.

* * *

As with any collection of ghost stories, the tales of Chama are met with a spectrum of belief and skepticism.

-**Natural Explanations**: Skeptics argue that the mysterious sounds and sights could be attributed to natural phenomena, quirks of old buildings, or the power of suggestion and imagination.

-**Cultural Legacy**: Believers and storytellers, on the other hand, see these tales as a vital part of Chama's cultural heritage, a link to the past that adds depth and intrigue to the town.

The Ghosts of Chama stand as a testament to the town's rich history and the enduring power of storytelling. Whether one believes in the spectral residents or not, the tales add a layer of mystery and charm to this small New Mexican town. For hikers on the CDT, a stop in Chama offers not just rest and resupply, but a chance to step into a world where the past lingers, and the echoes of yesteryear are heard in the whispers of the wind through the high country.

Conclusion

As I reflect upon the remarkable journey we've taken through the pages of *Legends and Stories: From the Continental Divide Trail*, my heart swells with gratitude for the opportunity to share this remarkable adventure with you, our fellow trailblazers and seekers of the extraordinary.

Our exploration of the Continental Divide Trail (CDT) has been a tapestry woven with tales of rugged landscapes and the indomitable human spirit. From the southern deserts of New Mexico, where the trail begins its ascent, to the remote wilderness of Glacier National Park in Montana, where it finds its end, we've traversed a world where the ordinary blurs into the extraordinary and where the ancient melds seamlessly with the modern.

But perhaps most importantly, we've ventured into the

heart of the unknown, delving into the unexplained phenomena, mysteries, and eerie stories that have fascinated generations of adventurers. From the ghostly lights of La Garita Wilderness to the haunting encounters within the San Juan Mountains, we've touched upon the inexplicable, reminding us that even in the most well-explored corners of our world, there remain enigmas that continue to captivate and mystify.

As you close the pages of this book and reflect on our collective journey, I hope you carry with you the spirit of adventure and the awareness that every trail, every bend in the path, has a story to tell. Whether you're inspired to embark on your own odyssey along the CDT or content to savor the tales from the comfort of your armchair, know that the wilderness is a tapestry of legends and stories, waiting for each of us to explore and discover.

In closing, I extend my heartfelt thanks for sharing in this adventure with us. May the stories within these pages continue to inspire, intrigue, and kindle your love for the great outdoors. As you step out into the world, remember that the legends of the Continental Divide Trail are not confined to its rugged terrain but live on in the footsteps of those who dare to explore and in the imaginations of all who seek the wonders of the wild.

- Steve Stockton

* * *

CONTINUE WITH
STEVE'S OTHER GREAT BOOKS

About the Author

Steve Stockton is a veteran outdoorsman and author who has been investigating the unexplained for over 35 years. Originally from the mountains of East Tennessee, Steve has traveled all over the country and many parts of the world and now makes his home in picturesque New England with his wife, Nicole, and their dog, Mulder.

Steve cites his influences as his "gypsy witch" grandmother, who told him multitudes of legends and stories as a small child, as well as authors such as Frank Edwards, John Keel, Charles Fort, Loren Coleman, Ivan Sanderson, Colin Wilson, and Nick Redfern.

His published books include Strange Things in the Woods (a collection of true, paranormal encounters) as well as the autobiographical My Strange World, where he talks about his own experiences dating back to childhood. Recently, he has written National Park Mysteries and Disappearances, Volumes 1, 2, and 3.

He also owns and narrates the wildly popular Among The Missing Youtube channel.

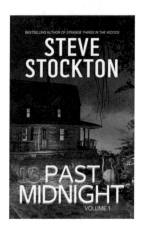

13 PAST MIDNIGHT SERIES

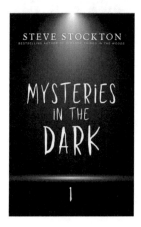

MYSTERIES IN THE DARK SERIES

STRANGE THINGS IN THE WOODS

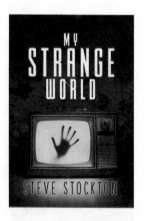

MY STRANGE WORLD

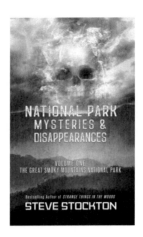

NATIONAL PARK MYSTERIES & DISAPPEARANCES SERIES

Also by Free Reign Publishing

THE WOODS: VOLUME 1

Made in the USA
Thornton, CO
07/08/24 16:54:50

81abd795-2661-4b94-87ae-d0dd718bd18aR01